# History of
# Monster
## Movies

**Timothy J. Bradley**

## ...sultants

**...mothy Rasinski, Ph.D.**
Kent State University

**Lori Oczkus, M.A.**
Literacy Consultant

### Publishing Credits

Rachelle Cracchiolo, M.S.Ed., *Publisher*
Conni Medina, M.A.Ed., *Managing Editor*
Dona Herweck Rice, *Series Developer*
Emily R. Smith, M.A.Ed., *Content Director*
Stephanie Bernard and Seth Rogers, *Editors*
Robin Erickson, *Multimedia Designer*

The TIME logo is a registered trademark of TIME Inc. Used under license.

**Image Credits:** cover, pp.1, 5, 6, 11, 12, 15, 25, 26 to 27, 31, 32, 35, 37, 42-43, 48 illustrations by Timothy J. Bradley; IBC, pp.10, 14, 20, 34 illustrations by Travis Hanson; pp.19, 28, 30, 40-41 illustrations by J.J. Rudisill; pp.7, 36 Moviestore collection Ltd / Alamy; p.8 John Kobal Foundation/Getty Images; p.9 Pictorial Press Ltd / Alamy; pp.13, 23, 31 AF archive / Alamy; p.16 Travis Hanson/Timothy J. Bradley; p.17 ZUMA Press, Inc. / Alamy; p.18 Wikimedia Commons/Public Domain; pp.21,41 Photos 12 / Alamy; p.24 Universal Pictures/Getty Images; p.29 Production Cos.: Carolco Pictures/Pacific Western Productions/ Lightstorm Entertainment/Le Studio Canal+ S.A./Still photographer: Zade Rosenthal/Atlaspix / Alamy; p.33 Koichi Kamoshida/Getty Images; pp.38-39 Timothy J. Bradley/Evan Ferrell; All other images from iStock and/or Shuterstock.

**Notes:** Readers should have parental permission before viewing the movies mentioned in this book due to possible mature themes or images. All characters and movies mentioned in this book are registered trademarks of their respective owners or developers and are used in this book strictly for editorial purposes. No commercial claim to their use is made by the author or the publisher.

### Library of Congress Cataloging-in-Publication Data

Names: Bradley, Timothy J. author.
Title: History of monster movies / Timothy J. Bradley.
Description: Huntington Beach, CA : Teacher Created Materials, 2016. | Includes index.
Identifiers: LCCN 2016012205 (print) | LCCN 2016023295 (ebook) | ISBN 9781493835966 (pbk.) | ISBN 9781480757004 (eBook)
Subjects: LCSH: Monster films--History and criticism--Juvenile literature. | Monsters in motion pictures--Juvenile literature.
Classification: LCC PN1995.9.M6 B83 2016 (print) | LCC PN1995.9.M6 (ebook) |
    DDC 791.43/67--dc23
LC record available at https://lccn.loc.gov/2016012205

### Teacher Created Materials

5301 Oceanus Drive
Huntington Beach, CA 92649-1030
http://www.tcmpub.com

**ISBN 978-1-4938-3596-6**

© 2017 Teacher Created Materials, Inc.
Made in China.
Nordica.062017.CA21700643

# Table of Contents

# Coming Attractions:
# What's a Monster Movie?

Picture it: you're munching on your popcorn, waiting expectantly for the film to begin. The lights in the theater dim. The film starts, and you witness a fearsome creature destroying an entire city. Buildings explode. Bridges are knocked over. People run screaming from a horrible creature bent on destroying everything in sight.

Relax, no reason to panic. It's just a monster movie!

The history of monster movies is a long and fascinating one. Many of us enjoy good scary films. Monster movies have evolved since their beginnings. Improvements in filmmaking and technology have allowed for new creatures to exist and new stories to be told. So, grab that popcorn and a good friend to hide behind, and get ready to explore monster movies from the very beginning.

## Tools of the Trade

The first motion picture cameras date back to the late 1880s. Early movie cameras had many limitations. The earliest films were only a minute long and didn't feature color or sound.

4

# The Beginning of
# Monster Movies (1915)

The German movie *The Golem* was one of the first monster movies ever produced. At that time, film was a new form of entertainment. Monster movies were an obvious fit to excite and engage audiences.

*The Golem* tells of a giant clay statue in the shape of a man that is brought to life. Golem finds itself misunderstood and goes on a killing rampage. The monster is portrayed by an actor in a suit with makeup on his face to resemble a being made of clay. From the very beginning, monster movies and theater makeup have been a thrilling pair!

Golem

## Fooling Your Brain

"Motion pictures" are in reality thousands and thousands of still images, or frames. The still images are shown rapidly in consecutive order. The images are shown at 24 frames per second. This fools your brain into thinking it is watching a single image of moving objects!

# Reel One:
# Human Meets Monster

Moviemakers realized that they could create stories that couldn't happen in the real world. They started to explore creepier subjects, and audiences went wild for them.

## *Nosferatu* (1922)

The film *Nosferatu* was adapted closely from Bram Stoker's novel *Dracula*. The film is **lauded** for the way it notches up creeping dread through the use of dramatic light and shadow. Max Schreck plays the vampire, Count Orlok. Even by today's movie standards, he is plenty creepy. Every vampire film made since then follows the trail of blood blazed by *Nosferatu*.

# Frankenstein (1931)

Another very popular book that was adapted into a monster movie is *Frankenstein*. Author Mary Shelley published her novel in 1818. She was 20 years old. Her story tells of a scientist who jolts a dead human body back to life.

Shelley's story sparked many films. The most popular one stars Boris Karloff as Dr. Frankenstein's monster. Even though the creature is killed at the end of the film, his popularity lives on. There have been many **sequels** and **reboots**.

## Science Gone Bad

*Frankenstein* has an important meaning. At its heart, it shows that science can lead to horrific consequences if it is used recklessly. Thankfully, most scientists in real life do their best to use science to make lives better and to teach others.

## *Dracula* (1931)

In another film version of Stoker's novel, Bela Lugosi was cast as the title vampire. His performance became **iconic**.

The film follows the bloodthirsty vampire from his castle in Transylvania to London. A scientist named Van Helsing tracks him down. Van Helsing pounds a wooden stake through Dracula's heart.

The film terrified audiences. In fact, newspapers reported that several audience members passed out from fear!

### Real Bloodsucking Monsters

There are several real-life creatures that feed on blood to survive! Vampire bats, leeches, ticks, *lampreys*, mosquitoes, and parasitic **isopods** all consume blood for food.

# King Kong (1933)

The giant ape called Kong was the creation of filmmaker Merian C. Cooper. The film *King Kong* follows an expedition to the mysterious Skull Island. The explorers discover prehistoric creatures roaming the island. They also encounter Kong. He is the most powerful creature on the island. Kong is captured and brought back to New York. But he escapes and goes on a rampage through the city.

*King Kong* is a masterpiece of stop-motion animation. The amazing effects astounded audiences. A 2005 version of *King Kong* uses computer graphics to create the monstrous ape and terrorize audiences.

## One Big Ape

There is actually a real species of prehistoric ape that was huge, although not quite as big as King Kong. *Gigantopithecus* went extinct about 100,000 years ago. This **herbivorous** ape grew to almost 10 feet (3 meters) and weighed about half a ton (454 kilograms)!

# The Wolf Man (1941)

Legends of **werewolves** have existed in Europe for hundreds of years. The film *The Wolf Man* brings those legends to the movie screen. When it was first released, it was a huge hit with audiences.

Actor Lon Chaney Jr. plays a man who is bitten by a wolf. Unfortunately, the wolf is actually a werewolf. The bite causes the man to change into a ferocious wolf whenever the moon is full.

The special effects to create the Wolf Man's change from man to wolf took about ten hours to prepare and film each time. Those hours translate to ten seconds in the final film.

## Werewolves in Real Life?!?

Werewolves are not real creatures. They are based on myth and legend. However, there is a real medical condition called **lycanthropy**. It occurs when a person has the delusion that he or she is a wolf or another animal.

# The Beast from 20,000 Fathoms (1953)

A short story by science-fiction writer Ray Bradbury serves as the basis for one of the most famous monsters from the 1950s. In the film *The Beast from 20,000 Fathoms*, a fictional dinosaur called *Rhedosaurus* escapes from Arctic ice. An atomic bomb test frees the creature. Ray Harryhausen brings the monster to life through stop-motion animation. Harryhausen had learned his craft by working closely with Willis O'Brien, the animator from *King Kong*. The result is an amazing monster movie.

## The Real Rhedosaurus

A real-life creature may have inspired the monster in Bradbury's story. The **Elasmosaurus** was a marine reptile with a long neck, a small head, and flippers. It lived during the late Cretaceous period. The reptile grew to be almost 50 feet (15 meters) long!

# THEM! (1954)

An atomic bomb was successfully tested at White Sands, New Mexico, in 1945. The weapon was used on Japan at the end of World War II. People all over the world were horrified by the destruction of nuclear blasts. Many countries raced to create their own stockpiles of atomic weapons. But the lingering effects of atom bomb blasts weren't fully understood. And the long-term results of **radiation** were unknown.

*THEM!* tells the story of a nest of gigantic ants. They undergo mutation due to the **fallout** from the White Sands atomic testing. The military finally battles the huge mutants through storm drains in Los Angeles.

The movie was very popular and sparked many giant bug films. The films that followed used the formula created by *THEM!* as a guide.

## Just as Dangerous

Bullet ants are just as dangerous, in their own way, as the ants in *THEM!*. They have the most painful stings in the insect world. Bullet ant stings have been compared to gun shots.

# *Godzilla* (1954)

Another radiation-based monster movie was made in Japan. Ishirō Honda directed a film about a giant reptilian monster. Radioactive fallout of atom-bomb tests mutates the monster. Godzilla stomps out of the sea to crash through the city of Tokyo. Everything in its path is destroyed. Godzilla is like the energy released in an atomic blast. Military weapons prove useless against the power of atoms being split apart.

Godzilla

## An Immortal Monster

Godzilla has been featured in about 30 films, with more installments in development.

# Reel Two:
# Monster Scares Human

The 1950s and 1960s marked the start of space programs around the world. This created a space race between countries. Satellites and rockets began to explore beyond our planet. Monster movies helped people imagine life in the unknown on this planet and beyond.

## Creature from the Black Lagoon (1954)

*Creature from the Black Lagoon* features a **humanoid** monster mutant who can survive underwater. The film tells the story of an archaeological expedition into the jungle. It attracts a curious gill man. The gill man wants to watch the explorers. But the creature frightens the humans. So, the humans attack him, but the gill man fights back.

The creature appears to die at the end of the film. But there were two sequels made. The gill man has become one of the iconic creatures of 1950s monster movies.

# It Came from Beneath the Sea (1955)

Ray Harryhausen's stop-motion animation skills were a huge hit with movie fans. *It Came from Beneath the Sea* became one of his most memorable films. In it, a giant octopus ensnares a submarine. The creature is attracted to the sub's nuclear engine.

The huge **cephalopod** menaces the San Francisco coastline and pulls down part of the Golden Gate Bridge. This animation was difficult and expensive to make in those days. To save time and money, Harryhausen made an octopus with just six limbs!

## Brainy Cephalopods

Real octopuses are very intelligent. They can learn, solve problems, and use tools to catch their prey! They can also **mimic** the colors and textures of their surroundings.

15

# *Forbidden Planet* (1956)

The space race among several nations led to questions about what might be found in space. Alien worlds became popular subjects for exciting movies.

*Forbidden Planet* follows the crew of a spacecraft. The crew is trying to connect with a human colony on the fourth planet of the star Altair. They find out that the colonists have been killed. The only survivors are a scientist, his daughter, and a robot named Robby. The crew realizes that the alien creature that killed the colonists is now hunting them. The monster is invisible. Only its tracks can be seen. It becomes visible when it passes through the crew's force field or is hit by weapon blasts.

A professional cartoon artist created the creature, or "Creature from the Id." The finished film effect is quite creepy.

## The Future of Music

The soundtrack for *Forbidden Planet* was generated using an electronic musical instrument called a **theremin**. To play a theremin, the musician holds his or her hands over loops of wire. Sound is made by moving the hands. The weird, electronic tones are the perfect soundtrack to the otherworldly setting of *Forbidden Planet*.

# The Deadly Mantis (1957)

The giant-ant movie *THEM!* sparked a whole colony of imitation films trying to cash in on its success while upping the scare factor. An insect destined to have its own giant-bug movie was the praying mantis. With its fierce appearance and voracious eating habits, the mantis is a terror.

In *The Deadly Mantis*, a huge mantis is freed from North Pole ice. It brings disaster wherever it goes. The giant insect was created using a puppet and miniature sets. It is thought that the sound that was used for the huge mantis was a lion's roar.

## Mantid Ancestor

Mantids can trace their ancestors back 300 million years. There is an old insect called the *Archimylacris*. It led to today's mantids, termites, and roaches.

# Beginning of the End (1957)

When one type of film is a success, copycat films get made. But the copycat films typically don't share the vision of the original film.

The *Beginning of the End* was, in fact, the beginning of the end of the giant-bug **genre**. The movie is about a scientist who grows huge wheat crops from **irradiated** seeds. A swarm of locusts eats the wheat. They, too, become giants. The movie uses real grasshoppers crawling on photos of buildings to create the effects. But it is not frightening. The movie is largely considered below the standard of earlier bug films.

# 20 Million Miles to Earth (1957)

Another space creature to star in its own monster movie is Ymir. This creature is an animal that is picked up during a space expedition to the planet Venus in the film *20 Million Miles to Earth*. Ymir starts off as a cute little hatchling but rapidly grows huge enough to endanger Earth.

Ray Harryhausen brought the alien Ymir to life through stop-motion animation. His skill at creating monsters and combining them with filmed actors was legendary. Audiences flocked to any film he worked on to see his creations come to life.

## Location, Location, Location!

Ray Harryhausen chose Italy as the location for *20 Million Miles to Earth* because he wanted to vacation there.

# *Jason and the Argonauts* (1963)

What's better than a monster movie? A movie with a *bunch* of monsters!

Greek mythology is a great source for movie material. The film *Jason and the Argonauts* is based on some well-known myths. The story follows Jason as he embarks on a quest for the Golden Fleece, which will be a sign of his right to rule the land he'd been forced to escape.

Harryhausen outdid himself with this film. The live actors battle a gang of skeletons, a hydra, and the giant bronze man, Talos.

## Stop-Motion Blockbuster

Harryhausen considered *Jason and the Argonauts* to be his best work. He combined several animated characters with live actors. Each shot was carefully **choreographed**.

## *Fantastic Voyage* (1966)

To bring new life to the monster-movie genre, filmmakers began to cross monster stories with science fiction. *Fantastic Voyage* is a science-fiction movie that features a very unusual monster. A submarine crew is shrunk to the size of a cell. The tiny sub is injected into the body of a scientist who has had a serious brain injury. The team has only 60 minutes before they—and the sub—will return to normal size. Inside the brain, the sub starts to revert to its full size and is attacked by a white blood cell. These cells are part of the body's defense against bacteria. After attacking the sub, the cell goes after the crew, and they have to find a way out of the body before they are attacked!

### The Perfect Man for the Job

The director of *Fantastic Voyage*, Richard Fleischer, took pre-med courses in college. These classes must have come in handy when working on the film!

# Scare Tactics

How much do you like to be scared? Here's a rundown of the "scare factor" for some of the films discussed in this book. One lit bulb means least scary; five lit bulbs means sleep in your parents' room!

**Beginning of the End**
**Dracula**

**Nosferatu**
**The Wolf Man**
**20 Million Miles to Earth**

**Frankenstein**
**King Kong**
**Creature from the Black Lagoon**
**It Came from Beneath the Sea**
**The Deadly Mantis**

**Godzilla (1954)**
**Forbidden Planet**
**Jason and the Argonauts**
**Independence Day**
**Lake Placid**
**THEM!**
**Pacific Rim**

*Godzilla (2014)*
*The Terminator*
*Pitch Black*
*Alien*
*I Am Legend*
*Cloverfield*
*The Thing*

# *The Andromeda Strain* (1971)

The possible dangers raised by the exploration of space during the 1960s were the basis of a novel by **Michael Crichton**. The book became the film *The Andromeda Strain*.

The monster in the film is an alien microorganism. It kills humans in seconds by turning all the blood in their bodies to powder. A staff of doctors in an underground lab races against time to find a cure for the deadly virus. Luckily, the lab comes with an atomic self-destruct device that is meant to stop the spread of the disease. Unfortunately, the device could cause the virus to mutate and spread out of control!

## Idea Man

Crichton was a medical doctor, movie director, and writer of screenplays as well as novels and short stories. He also wrote the very popular novel *Jurassic Park*.

# The Food of the Gods (1976)

This monster movie is based on a story by H. G. Wells about possible dangerous outcomes to scientific experiments. At the time of its release, this was a growing concern in the real world.

In the film, the food of the gods comes out of the ground on a remote island. Rats and wasps eat it and grow to huge sizes. Then, they attack the islanders. The animals are finally killed, but the mysterious food drifts to a mainland farm. The dairy cows ingest the food, and children drink the milk from the cows. The children will presumably start growing to giant size.

## Ahead of His Time

Wells is a popular 19th century author. He is best known for his science-fiction novels such as *The Time Machine*, *The Invisible Man*, and *The War of the Worlds*. These have all been adapted into films several times each!

# Reel Three:
# Human Battles Monster

As space programs continued to expand and sometimes proved deadly, monster movies began to look deeper at the dark side of venturing into space and into other unknown worlds.

## *Alien* (1979)

*Alien* set a new standard for modern movie monsters. On the surface, the film is a simple story of a monster aboard a spacecraft. That plot has been used since the 1950s. It might seem overdone. But there are two major differences with *Alien*. The director, Ridley Scott, used his talents to bring a rusted, industrial look to the spacecraft. And designer H. R. Giger created a unique and frightening creature for the movie. It was made by **fabricating** a suit for an actor to wear. Scott's use of light and shadow keeps the audience wondering what the creature looks like. The suspense is almost more than audiences can take!

*Alien* became a huge success. It even inspired many copycat films and creatures.

### Acting Like an Alien

Six-foot ten-inch (2.08 meters) Bolaji Badejo is the actor inside the creature suit in *Alien*. The combination of his height and the creature suit is what gives the monster its spindly, insect-like look.

## Titanic Tugboat

Most of the action in *Alien* takes place aboard a "space tug," which is towing a huge ore refinery back to Earth. It is full of expensive resources. Such tugs have been considered for bringing icy comets to Earth as water sources or asteroids for their mineral resources.

## STOP! THINK...

Use the illustration of the Alien creature to answer these questions:

- What features make the Alien creature so menacing?

- What changes could be made to the creature to alter it from menacing to friendly?

27

# The Thing (1982)

When director John Carpenter's film *The Thing* opened in theaters, audiences were stunned by the ultra-gory effects. The tone of the film was bleak, and the initial public response was hostile. The film produced low ticket sales. Years later, when it was released on video, *The Thing* gained cult status for its quirky characters and over-the-top alien effects.

*The Thing* is based on a science-fiction story written in 1938. "Who Goes There?," by John W. Campbell Jr., is about a shape-shifting alien astronaut frozen in Arctic ice. The alien is thawed by the staff of a scientific outpost. There, it starts to mimic and kill the men one by one.

## Love Your Work!

Rob Bottin, who created the effects for *The Thing*, worked on the film seven days a week for more than a year.

# The Terminator (1984)

James Cameron created a film about a killer robot—with a twist! *The Terminator* features a murderous robot sent back in time. Its mission is to kill the mother of the man who will liberate humans from the deadly machines in the future.

Stan Winston Studio created the film's special effects. Practical effects such as puppets were used. Some stop-motion animation was also used to portray the robot.

# Independence Day (1996)

Alien invader stories aren't anything new. But special effects have made some major leaps since the 1950s. Today's effects can handle any idea a director can dream up!

The story of *Independence Day* could have been written back in the 1950s. But it's the 1990s effects that make it amazing for audiences. The film follows an alien invasion that happens on an American holiday. Cities around the world are destroyed in the same instant by powerful weapons. A group of heroes must work to fight the aliens and save the day.

## THINK LINK

OK, so Earth isn't in danger of imminent attack by aliens. But, it's always good to plan ahead, right?

- ◎ What kind of defenses would you put into effect to be ready for an alien invasion?

- ◎ How would you figure out the best way to defeat the invaders? What weaknesses might they have?

- ◎ How could you set up an "early warning system" to let people on Earth know about an alien spaceship approaching the planet?

## Lake Placid (1999)

*Lake Placid* is an exciting film about a terrifying monster. The film's director builds a lot of humor into the story as well. The humor gives viewers a chance to catch their breath between scares. Many recent monster movies and horror films have touches of humor. These give the audiences momentary breaks from the terror.

In the film, a huge crocodile is loose in a fictional town in Maine. The town's sheriff and a scientist try to track down and capture the rampaging reptile. They learn that an elderly woman living at the edge of town has been feeding live cows to the giant crocodile. And it turns out that there are not one but *two* crocodiles in the lake!

scene from *Lake Placid*

### Build-It-Yourself Crocodile
Stan Winston Studio built a full-size, animated crocodile robot that was used in the film.

## *Pitch Black* (2000)

*Pitch Black* is set in the distant future. A transport spacecraft carrying a dangerous prisoner crash-lands. The planet the ship lands on has three suns. When the planet enters a total eclipse, its sky becomes completely dark. Deadly flying creatures emerge from underground caverns and fill the dark skies. The prisoner has excellent night vision. The most dangerous man on the ship is suddenly the only hope for everyone.

### Ping!

The fictional creatures in *Pitch Black* hunt by **echolocation**, just like bats do in the real world.

## *I, Robot* (2004)

Science-fiction author Isaac Asimov is famous for his robot stories. The film *I, Robot* combines some of his stories into an exciting movie. It tells of a police officer in Chicago in the future. He investigates a suicide that might be a murder … committed by a robot.

The film's realistic robots are made by special computer-generated effects. Actor Alan Tudyk plays the title robot. But it's his movements, not him, that are recorded by film. This is done through motion capture. Motion capture is when an actor wears a special body suit. Then, key physical points are marked on the suit. The points are transferred to the same locations on the virtual character that is being created. The virtual character is then animated using those key points. Motion capture marks a new wave of monster-movie development.

# I Am Legend (2007)

Zombie films made a huge comeback in the 2000s. An exciting addition to the zombie film genre is *I Am Legend*. The film is adapted from a story by Richard Matheson. It follows a doctor who stays in New York City after a zombie plague sweeps through. He tries to create a vaccine against the disease. He also must avoid the infected beings that live hidden in the city. They emerge each night to look for him.

## Reboot!

The story *I Am Legend* has been adapted into film three times. Each film updates the story and characters for new audiences.

## *Cloverfield* (2008)

*Cloverfield* is an update of the classic "creature features" from the 1950s and 1960s. It combines all the elements of old-time monster movies with new technology to make them even more realistic. This film uses the **found-footage** approach. The footage shows a giant creature rising from the ocean off the New York coast. A group of friends tries to escape before the military sends jets to bomb the monster and the city itself.

# Reel Four:
## Monster Destroys Planet

There has been a surge in new monster movies recently. That's because of the amazing leaps in special effects such as computer-generated imagery (CGI). Lifelike monsters are now more possible than ever.

## *Pacific Rim* (2013)

*Pacific Rim* features giant robots fighting giant monsters and creepy aliens. The aliens send monsters through a space-time rift to attack human cities. Humans build huge robots to fight back.

The robots and monsters in this film are all created by computers. There are fewer limitations in this method compared to using models or stop-motion. And characters can fight in dramatic fashions. That makes for an exciting movie!

# Godzilla (2014)

In the original *Godzilla*, Tokyo is destroyed and people run screaming all over the place. This film is a reboot of the 1954 black-and-white movie. But it uses modern film methods. The script also creates a new origin story for Godzilla. And the monster is even larger than in the original!

## A Real Animal

The way the new Godzilla fights is based on real animals, such as Komodo dragons and bears.

# End Credits:
# Making Monsters

To make a great monster movie, you need a monster. That's obvious. The tricky part is figuring out how to make it appear real on a movie screen—without blowing your budget!

There are three common ways to create believable monsters. They are *practical effects*, *CGI characters*, and *stop-motion animation*. Take a look at how each works and the effects each method creates.

## Practical Effects

Practical effects are built to appear and work on the set with the actors. Puppetry, makeup, scale models, and animatronics are some practical effects. An advantage to using them is that they give the actors something real to react to. With these effects, full-size creatures can appear on the sets along with the actors.

## CGI Characters

Today's technology makes it possible to build virtual creatures that are realistic. The creatures can be **composited** with live footage. Actors work with real or CGI sets to create scenes that may not exist in the real world.

# Stop-Motion Animation

Stop-motion animation is a simple concept. Turn the page to see how it's done!

Many people need to work together to bring a monster to the big screen.

# Stop-Motion Animation

1. Create a jointed **armature**.

2. Sculpt a rigid clay sculpture over the armature.

3. Use the sculpture to create molds or silicone casts of the movable parts for the monster.

4. Assemble the movable parts and paint the model monster.

5. Create the set, and set up the lights and camera.

6. Shoot a few frames of film of the monster on the set.

7. Move the model slightly. ——

8. Shoot a few frames of film. ——————

9. Move the model slightly again. ——

10. Shoot a few more frames of film. ——

11. Repeat steps 9–10 several hundred times until the movement is complete. ——

REPEAT

animation for *Frankenweenie*

# Rave Reviews:
# Watch Out!

Monster movies have come a long way since their beginnings, when audiences appreciated actors wearing monster costumes. Practical effects have brought countless popular monsters to the screen. Stop-motion animation was a breakthrough that still thrills movie audiences when done skillfully. And now, CGI has made possible anything that a film director can imagine. Giant scarecrows with laser vision? No problem. A heaving mass of killer zombies? Done. Entire cities flattening under a killer monster's terrifying rampage? Yeah, they've got that, too.

It's hard to imagine where moviemakers might go in the future. The advances that have been made so far suggest that even more amazing things are to come. And how much more realistic will audiences want their monster movies to get? Watch out!

## New Monsters

Many monster movies from the past were reflections of uneasiness about life. These movies included natural disasters or human-made threats, like atomic weapons. What new monsters will rise from our worries and fears?

## Coming Soon to a Theater Near You

What might new technologies bring to the movie-going experience? What if you could make a 3-D printed model of the monster from the movie you just watched? Or maybe have yourself projected into the movie as one of the characters evading a deadly creature?

# Glossary

**armature**—an inner structure used for puppets

**cephalopod** (SEF-uh-luh-pod)—the group of creatures to which octopuses and squid belong

**choreographed**—movements planned out in advance

**composited**—several different pieces of film sandwiched together into one

**consecutive**—happening one after the other

**echolocation**—a process for locating objects by sound waves

**Elasmosaurus** (ihl-az-muh-SAWR-uhs)—an extinct marine reptile with a long neck and four paddle-like limbs

**fabricating**—making or building something

**fallout**—radioactive particles in the atmosphere

**found-footage**—a visual style in which the film looks to have been shot with handheld video cameras

**genre**—a series of books or films that share a theme and style

**herbivorous** (huhr-BIV-uh-rus)—plant eating

**humanoid**—like a human

**iconic**—widely recognized as a symbol

**irradiated**—exposed to radiation

**isopods**—groups of crustaceans that have segmented shells and several pairs of legs

**lampreys** (LAM-preez)—eel-like fish that have round mouths full of rasping teeth

**lauded** (LAWD-ihd)—praised

**lycanthropy** (lahy-KAN-thruh-pee)—a condition that makes a person believe he or she is a wolf or other animal

**microorganism**—a tiny microscopic organism

**mimic**—copy

**radiation**—energy released by certain elements such as radium or uranium

**reboots**—retellings of stories in new ways

**sequels**—continuations of books or films

**silicone**—a rubbery substance that is used in making puppets for animation

**stop-motion animation**—a film technique in which a puppet is moved slightly, then filmed, then moved again

**theremin**—an electronic musical instrument

**werewolves**—mythical monsters that begin life as humans but change into wolves

# Index

# Check It Out!

## Books

Bradley, Timothy. 2013. *Infestation*. Scholastic.

_____. 2013. *Sci Hi: Hive Mind*. Argosy Press.

_____. 2014. *Sci Hi: Ripple Effect*. Argosy Press.

_____. 2014. *Sci Hi: Time Jump*. Argosy Press.

Harryhausen, Ray, and Tony Dalton. 2010. *Ray Harryhausen: An Animated Life*. Aurum Press.

_____. 2008. *A Century of Stop-Motion Animation: From Mélies to Ardman*. Watson-Guptill.

Jones, Stephen. 1999. *The Essential Monster Movie Guide*. Titan Books.

Landis, John. 2011. *Monsters in the Movies*. Dorling Kindersley.

Mallory, Michael. 2009. *Universal Studios Monsters: A Legacy of Horror*. Universe.

Rovin, Jeff. 1990. *Encyclopedia of Monsters*. Facts on File.

Shelley, Mary. 1994. *Frankenstein*. Dover Publications.

Stevenson, Robert Louis. 1991. *The Strange Case of Dr. Jekyll and Mr. Hyde*. Dover Publications.

Stoker, Bram. 2000. *Dracula*. Dover Publications.

Wells, H. G. 2012. *H. G. Wells: Six Novels*. Canterbury Classics.

## Websites

*The Official Ray Harryhausen Website*. http://www.rayharryhausen.com/.

# Try It!

Imagine that you're a sought-after film director and you've been offered *one hundred million dollars* to produce and direct a monster movie. You've got some decisions to make:

- ◎ Draw a picture or write a description of the monster your movie will be about.

- ◎ Decide what kind of special effects you will want to use (stop-motion animation, practical effects, or computer graphics).

- ◎ Plan some of the things you'll need to build or get for your monster movie to be filmed (sets, city miniatures, spacecraft models, special lighting, sculptures of the monster, buckets of slime or cobwebs, fog machines, and so on).

- ◎ If you're planning to use CGI characters, think about motion-capture computer software and hardware as well as computer-generated sets.

- ◎ Think about the backstory for your monster. Is it an alien from space? Is it a mad scientist's experiment gone wrong? A government project? Or maybe just a random mutation in nature that leads to a bloodthirsty, rampaging monster?

# About the Author

Tim Bradley grew up watching monster movies every Saturday afternoon. He would constantly draw monsters and prehistoric creatures, and he had so much fun that he decided to do it for a living! As a professional artist and author, Tim writes about the wild stuff of science and science fiction. He lives in sunny Southern California with his wife and son.

Tim's monster novel, *Infestation*, and his *Sci Hi* science-fiction trio (*Hive Mind, Ripple Effect*, and *Time Jump*) bring to life Tim's love of monsters and weird and wild possibilities!